ATOMIC WEDGIES, WET WILLIES,

& OTHER ACTS OF ROGUERY

GREG TANANBAUM
DAN MARTIN

ILLUSTRATIONS BY BRYAN DUDDLES

SANTA
MONICA
PRESS

Published by:
Santa Monica Press LLC
P.O. Box 1076
Santa Monica, CA 90406-1076
1-800-784-9553
www.santamonicapress.com
books@santamonicapress.com

Printed in the United States

Santa Monica Press books are available at special quantity discounts when purchased in bulk by corporations, organizations, or groups.
Please call our Special Sales department at 1-800-784-9553.

Library of Congress Cataloging-in-Publication Data

Tananbaum, Greg, 1971-
Atomic wedgies, wet willies & other acts of roguery : by greg tananbaum and dan martin.
  p. cm.
  ISBN 1-59580-000-X
  1. Amusements. 2. Tricks. I. Martin, Dan, 1970- II. Title.
  GV1201.T28 2005
  793--dc22
  2005001387

Cover and interior design by Future Studio.

CONTENTS

One Friday evening in the not too-distant past, we found ourselves driving to Lake Tahoe for a weekend ski trip. Having been unexpectedly stuck at work late that night, we were eager to make good time in order to catch up with the rest of our families who had left earlier in the day. Unfortunately, a flat tire on the side of the highway threw yet another wrench into our vacation plans and severely dampened our collective spirits. However, from the depths of darkness opportunity often comes, and this flat tire was no exception.

As Greg knelt down to set up the jack, Dan was struck by a simple thought: this was a perfect Atomic Wedgie situation! He harkened back to his youth, snuck up behind Greg, grabbed ahold of his underwear waistband, and let it rip. A few minutes later, after Greg's initial anger and embarrassment had begun to subside, he laughed at the thought of receiving his first Atomic Wedgie in over two decades. We began talking about similar pranks. As we had both grown up with older brothers, we had each experienced a huge number and variety of attacks. As summer camp attendees, we had each executed our share as well. As graduates of prestigious East Coast universities, we had heard a litany of prep school horror stories from blue-blooded roommates. One spare tire, half of a torn Fruit of the Loom underwear, and one hundred miles later, we arrived in Lake Tahoe, armed with a dream: "We," we said to ourselves and our incredulous wives, "are going to be the Wedgie Kings!"

The more we discussed it, the more we realized that nobody had ever bothered to catalogue the myriad pranks most kids encounter during their formative years. Some of the acts of roguery didn't even have a name, and we relished the opportunity to leave our mark on pop culture. Other acts possessed names and/or mutant strains that seemed to vary according to the regions in which they were perpetrated. A "Purple Nurple" in Philadelphia could easily be a "Texas Tornado" or "Titty Twister" in the Midwest. Aside from the names themselves, what intrigued us most about the acts of roguery were their sheer number and variety. Clearly, we had to make some sense of the madness.

In order to tackle the formidable challenge of compiling some 50-plus acts, we resorted to what any scientist would do when encountering way too much information: we set up a classification scheme. At first blush, the purpose of most rogue acts seemed to center on the infliction of physical pain. Upon closer inspection and experimentation, however, we concluded that the mental anguish felt by the victim could in many circumstances outweigh any physical harm.

In the end, we chose a flexible system that rated each act according to the pain, embarrassment, and annoyance felt by the victim. In calculating the overall score, we felt equal weighting should be given to each of the above categories as well as a fourth score that encompassed the difficulty of executing the act. A perfect "40," therefore, would be an act that was virtually impossible to pull off and which inflicted maximum pain, annoyance, and embarrassment to the victim.

Any rating system is useless, however, unless it provides the substance and content behind the ratings. In addition to the ratings for each act, *Atomic Wedgies, Wet Willies, & Other Acts of Roguery* also provides full descriptions, proper pronunciation, pointers, countermeasures, and a series of illustrations that should help any would-be Wedgie King achieve everlasting glory.

We hope you'll enjoy reading this book as much as our wives hated the entire concept.

Happy roguery to all!

GREG TANANBAUM and DAN MARTIN

WARNING

Participating in any act of roguery can involve significant risks of property damage, personal injury, humiliation, lost productivity, and other ailments too numerous and icky to mention. You should assess your own strength and dexterity as well as your opponent's prior to undertaking any of these rogue acts. If you find yourself relatively deficient in any one area, be prepared to face the consequences. Ratings of each rogue act are not vetted by any international standards body, and should be used for general guideline purposes only.

ATOMIC WEDGIE

PAIN	ANNOYANCE	EMBARRASSMENT	DIFFICULTY	TOTAL POINTS OUT OF 40
9	10	10	9	38

DEFINITION

Atomic Wedgie (*a-'tä-mik we-jE*): The action of pulling a person's underwear waistband from behind to a height approaching the shoulder blades.

TIPS FOR EXECUTION

☞ The Atomic Wedgie can succeed through either brute force or the element of surprise.

☞ When grabbing the victim's underwear, seek to execute a grip that includes both the waistband and the actual underwear material; this minimizes the risk that the band will tear off before atomic status is reached.

POSSIBLE COUNTERMEASURES

☞ If the attack comes from behind, step down hard on the assailant's foot, or elbow the assailant in the abdomen, stomach, or groin.

☞ For an intended victim with a martial arts background, attempt a judo throw by pushing backward, grabbing the assailant's arm, and flipping him over the shoulder.

☞ For a nonviolent defense, enjoy the liberating "al fresco" experience of life without underwear.

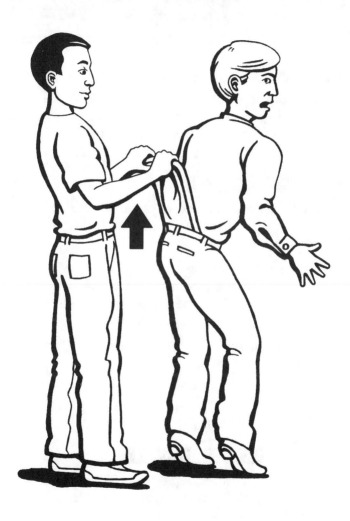

BOOK KNOCK

PAIN	ANNOYANCE	EMBARRASSMENT	DIFFICULTY	TOTAL POINTS OUT OF 40
1	6	6	4	17

DEFINITION

Book Knock (*buk näk*): Sneaking up behind a person who is carrying a stack of books, then pushing or pulling the books out of that person's hand so that they fall to the floor loudly and messily.

TIPS FOR EXECUTION

☞ The Book Knock is best executed in crowded hallways where the victim's embarrassment will be magnified by a larger audience.

☞ The Book Knock can be convincingly passed off as an accident; for example, pretending to trip or be pushed into the victim so that the books are "inadvertently" knocked (wink, wink) is a possibility.

☞ Alternatively, take pride in the act by shouting "book inspector!" right before knocking.

☞ For the true pro, wait for the Book Knockee to bend over to retrieve his fallen possessions, and then follow with a "Kick Me" Sign.

POSSIBLE COUNTERMEASURES

☞ A variety of outfitters (e.g., LL Bean, REI) market durable backpacks that eliminate the need to hand-carry books; consider investing in one.

☞If a backpack is undesirable or unfeasible, try carrying
   books with both arms, cradled against the chest.
   Note: if a passerby asks to see the stack of books,
   do not look down, as he may be preparing to execute
   a Nose Tweak.

BUBBLE BOWL

PAIN	ANNOYANCE	EMBARRASSMENT	DIFFICULTY	TOTAL POINTS OUT OF 40
1	7	5	1	14

DEFINITION

Bubble Bowl (*bub-bl bOl*): Pouring a generous amount of dish soap into the toilet bowl so that when a person urinates bubbles form in great quantities and spill over the toilet seat.

TIPS FOR EXECUTION

☞ Be very generous with the amount of liquid soap poured into the bowl, as a too-small quantity will lead to minimal sudsing which may be easily confused with normal urinary froth.

☞ To increase the Annoyance rating, choose a colored brand of dish soap, which may give the victim the mistaken fear of a kidney or bladder infection.

POSSIBLE COUNTERMEASURES

☞ Male victims should be able to see the building wall of bubbles; attempting a mid-stream cutoff may be a painful but necessary step.

☞ Female victims have no such visual advantage and must rely on the sense of touch as a warning system; unfortunately, if the bubbles have risen to such a level that they touch the victim's backside, the damage has already been done.

BUBBLE BOWL

☞ Do not attempt to flush the toilet, as the water-swirl will only further agitate the froth. If a bowl brush or plunger is available, simply stir the bubbled water until the suds disappear. With any luck, the next bathroom occupant will become the victim.

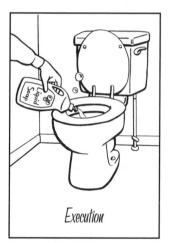

Execution

Result

BURP 'N' BLOW

PAIN	ANNOYANCE	EMBARRASSMENT	DIFFICULTY	TOTAL POINTS OUT OF 40
2	9	3	3	17

DEFINITION

Burp 'n' Blow (*burp N blO*): Belching and blowing the expelled air forcefully in the direction of a person's face.

TIPS FOR EXECUTION

☞ Enjoy foods containing onions, garlic, foreign cheeses, or other pungent ingredients.

☞ To accelerate a burp, drink a carbonated beverage as quickly as possible, gulping air in between sips; this is known as "Mr. Pibbing it."

☞ When a belch is imminent, entice the victim to lean forward by pretending to share a secret.

☞ Aim the burp itself directly at the victim's nose, and be sure to blow hard enough to envelope his entire head in a putrid bubble. If the expulsion is large enough, it is quite possible the victim will be forced to inhale multiple gulps of the foul odor.

POSSIBLE COUNTERMEASURES

☞ Avoid offers to hear a secret from someone who fits the Burp 'n' Blow profile (soda drinker, smelly food eater, etc.).

☞ Practice burping at will to develop a forceful response. Most perpetrators are not expecting an immediate counterstrike; this defensive burp volley will up the ante.

☞ As the perpetrator is likely to come in close with the blow, throw down a Head Butt or Noogie.

CARPET TUG

PAIN	ANNOYANCE	EMBARRASSMENT	DIFFICULTY	TOTAL POINTS OUT OF 40
8	8	8	10	34

DEFINITION

Carpet Tug (*kärpit tug*): The act of rapidly pulling a carpet with such force so as to send a person standing on it reeling backward.

TIPS FOR EXECUTION

☞ The Carpet Tug works best with long, skinny rugs typically found in hallways—large rugs are too heavy to jerk rapidly and small rugs provide insufficient surface area to lift.

☞ The victim should be far away from the "grabbing" edge, but not so far that he can step off the end (the "free" edge) as soon as he feels the carpet begin to move. Optimal distance is two-thirds to three-quarters of the way to the "free" edge.

☞ When using a new carpet, consider testing it first on a pet dog or cat. Add weight gradually until you match the weight of the intended victim (sand bags are an excellent prop in this regard).

☞ To build up necessary slack and speed, first push the carpet toward the victim before reversing direction and pulling it hard in the opposite direction.

☞ For heavier carpets requiring one accomplice on each end of the carpet, practice hand signs, winks, or other gestures as the "go" signal.

CARPET TUG

☞ Secure all freestanding rugs in the house; the town carpeteer should have a wide range of tapes, rubber mats, and other skid-reducing materials.

☞ Avoid large-knotted, handicraft wool rugs, which tend to slide much easier than their small-knotted, artificial counterparts.

☞ For frequent problem areas, consider installing handrails or safety straps.

CHAIR YANK

PAIN	ANNOYANCE	EMBARRASSMENT	DIFFICULTY	TOTAL POINTS OUT OF 40
9	9	8	3	29

DEFINITION

Chair Yank (*cher ya[ng]k*): The removal of a person's chair just as that person is preparing to sit down, causing the victim to fall to the floor.

TIPS FOR EXECUTION

☞ Timing is the critical component for success; the quick draw back of the chair must occur only after the victim begins downward descent, as noted by the bend in the victim's knees.

☞ A full draw back of the chair will help ensure that the victim does not catch any piece of the chair seat with the hand or arm (a "partial").

☞ The scrape of chair legs as they are dragged across the floor will serve to alert potential victim; lift the chair, or execute only on carpeted surfaces that muffle dragging sounds.

☞ Remain outside of the field of vision, typically by crouching behind the victim and ensuring that no mirrors are in the direct vicinity.

CHAIR YANK

POSSIBLE COUNTERMEASURES

☞ As much as practical, look behind your chair prior to sitting.

☞ Maintain at least one hand in constant contact with your chair during descent.

☞ Keep knees fully locked during descent until connection with seat is made. Note: this requires developed buttocks and hamstrings so exercise may be necessary.

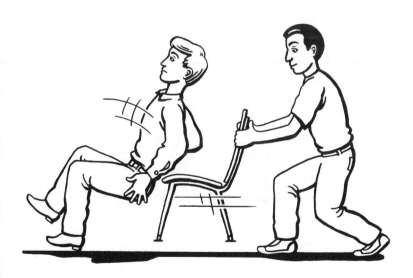

CHARLEY HORSE

PAIN	ANNOYANCE	EMBARRASSMENT	DIFFICULTY	TOTAL POINTS OUT OF 40
10	10	2	8	30

DEFINITION

Charley Horse (*chär-lE hors*): Striking a victim with a closed fist in the arm or leg in such a way that the middle knuckle of the middle finger causes numbness, then intense pain, in a tightly located area; also known as dead leg or dead arm.

TIPS FOR EXECUTION

☞ Aim for the side of the thigh or arm, not the topmost, fleshier area. If the intended target area is the leg, aim for mid-thigh, just in front of standard American and European pants inseams.

☞ Maintain a straight wrist and drive down from directly above the target area, so as to avoid a "recoil effect" that will injure the assailant.

☞ Strike quickly, with force, and seek to bury the knuckle as close to the bone as possible.

☞ Attacking seated or prostrate victims is preferable to attacking standing victims (a.k.a. The Lord Charles). If victim is standing, target the leg that is bearing the majority of the victim's weight.

CHARLEY HORSE

☞ Seated victims may need to be immobilized; the best technique to accomplish this is to first push the victim sideways and then immobilize both legs by sitting on the knees.

☞ An ideal target is a person watching TV, eating, or otherwise engaged alone in the middle of a three-person or larger sofa.

Target Areas

CHARLEY HORSE

POSSIBLE COUNTERMEASURES

☞ When watching TV, eating, or otherwise engaging in solo activities, sit in a single-person chair.

☞ If a sectional couch is the only seating option, try standing; should this not be feasible, sit on one side of the couch and use the arm of the sofa to help guard the outside leg.

☞ Should an attack occur, roll onto your stomach or back to protect sensitive areas, and keep legs in motion to prevent the perpetrator from landing a square strike (the "egg beater" defense).

☞ If prone to attack, consider thermal underwear for extra insulation to deaden the blow; in warmer (i.e., shorts) weather, apply extra sunscreen to target areas, which should cause any strike to slide off more easily and reduce damage.

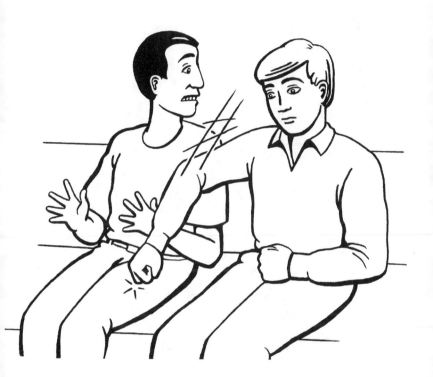

Execution

CLAP TRAP

PAIN	ANNOYANCE	EMBARRASSMENT	DIFFICULTY	TOTAL POINTS OUT OF 40
1	6	10	6	23

DEFINITION

Clap Trap (*klap trap*): Typically executed at a speech, assembly, or other public gathering; the action of starting a round of applause at an inappropriate time, thus enticing another person to clap; the initiator of the applause then ceases and stares at the second person as if in disbelief.

TIPS FOR EXECUTION

☞ Select a victim seated nearby, and clap at a low volume so that only those in closest proximity can hear. This is essential in selling the disbelief in the final stage of the act.

☞ Lead applause at a few appropriate moments in order to build the victim's trust.

☞ Look at the still-clapping victim with utter disgust and encourage others to do the same.

POSSIBLE COUNTERMEASURES

☞ Use personal judgment when applauding; do not simply follow the lead of the person in the next seat.

☞ Refrain from clapping until a critical mass of the audience has joined in.

CLAP TRAP

Execution

Result

COIN FLIP

PAIN	ANNOYANCE	EMBARRASSMENT	DIFFICULTY	TOTAL POINTS OUT OF 40
1	3	5	2	11

DEFINITION

Coin Flip (*koin flip*): Gluing a coin to the ground and watching as unsuspecting victims struggle in vain to pick it up.

TIPS FOR EXECUTION

☞ Use a strong, clear adhesive such as Instant Krazy Glue to spot weld the coin to the ground.

☞ A common mistake is to use a penny; avoid this at all costs, as few people these days stop to pick up such small change.

☞ The Coin Flip is best executed outdoors; gluing anything to a friend's or family member's floor generally demonstrates bad form.

☞ Try to place the coin in high traffic areas that can be easily and inconspicuously observed, such as in front of a gumball machine, outside of a Starbuck's, or on the stairs of the local courthouse.

☞ If you're feeling particularly playful, approach the victim as he is bending over, say something banal like "Your lucky day, huh?" Then, give him a pat on the back while applying a "Kick Me" Sign.

COIN FLIP

POSSIBLE COUNTERMEASURES

☞ Avoid picking up loose change unless in desperate need of money; the potential loss of dignity costs a lot more than a nickel or quarter.

☞ Try to gently kick the coin before bending to pick it up; if the coin doesn't move, just keep on walking.

Execution

Result

DOOR JAM

PAIN	ANNOYANCE	EMBARRASSMENT	DIFFICULTY	TOTAL POINTS OUT OF 40
1	3	6	8	18

DEFINITION

Door Jam (*dur jam*): Pretending to be hit in the face by a door in such a way that the person who has just walked through the doorway is believed to have caused the slam.

TIPS FOR EXECUTION

☞ Follow the prospective victim into the doorframe at close proximity, and knock a foot or knee into the bottom of the door. The noise should cause the victim to turn around.

☞ Wearing heavy shoes will increase the decibel level of the door kick and make the incident appear more dramatic.

☞ Immediately shielding the face with the hands as if in extreme distress should heighten the effect.

☞ For professional-level execution, carry a ketchup packet and tear upon impact to simulate a nosebleed.

POSSIBLE COUNTERMEASURES

☞ As a general rule of etiquette, holding the door both demonstrates good manners and thwarts prospective Door Jammers.

☞ If presented with the option, use a revolving door instead of the traditional variety. Note: this leaves open the possibility of the Revolving Door Hold.

☞ If jammery is suspected, raise the stakes by pretending to call 911; this should separate the rogue from the legitimate trauma victim.

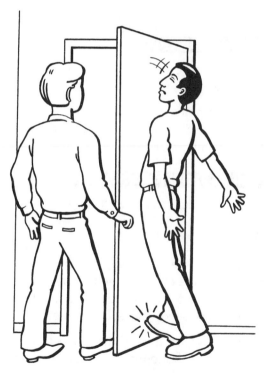

DUTCH OVEN

PAIN	ANNOYANCE	EMBARRASSMENT	DIFFICULTY	TOTAL POINTS OUT OF 40
2	9	2	6	19

DEFINITION

Dutch Oven (*duch o-ven*): Farting while sharing a bed with a sleeping partner, followed by the pulling of the bed covers over the partner's head, so as to trap the partner in the sealed gas pocket.

TIPS FOR EXECUTION

☞ Wait until the victim is dozing so that his response time and reflexes are slowed.

☞ Roll on top of the victim to lock him in a prone position; note that this will trap both parties in the Dutch Oven (a.k.a. The Holland Tunnel).

POSSIBLE COUNTERMEASURES

☞ The simplest defense against the Dutch Oven is to sleep alone.

☞ If sharing a bed is desirable or unavoidable, tuck both the covers on the side of the bed furthest from the assailant and the covers at the foot of the bed in tightly; this should make it difficult for the assailant to acquire the necessary bedding to cover the victim's head.

☞ If you are trapped in the Dutch Oven, crawl to freedom at the bottom of or the side of the bed.

DUTCH OVEN

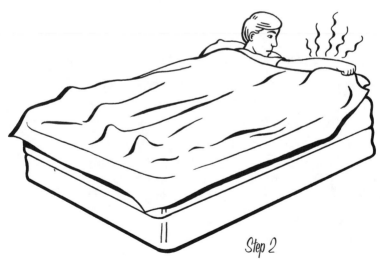

ESKIMO HOOK

PAIN	ANNOYANCE	EMBARRASSMENT	DIFFICULTY	TOTAL POINTS OUT OF 40
10	9	8	10	37

DEFINITION

Eskimo Hook (*es-ke-'mO huk*): The act of standing behind or beside a person and placing one or both index fingers inside a person's mouth, pulling outward on the cheeks as forcefully as possible.

TIPS FOR EXECUTION

☞ The element of surprise is crucial. Furthermore, so is the element of the victim's mouth being open.

☞ To maximize both elements, sneak up behind a talking person.

☞ Slowly move both index fingers around the victim's head, then very quickly insert them into the mouth.

☞ Pull outward and backward immediately, before the victim's bite reflex takes over and crushes the index fingers.

☞ For a side strike (The Siberian), secure the victim in a headlock similar to pre-Noogie positioning. As the victim starts to scream, insert only one finger and pull backwards and upwards on the cheek.

ESKIMO HOOK

POSSIBLE COUNTERMEASURES

☞ If the perpetrator does not get a clean insertion into the mouth, biting down hard may end the assault.

☞ A reverse Head Butt should serve to break the hook grip.

☞ Cheeks are surprisingly strong; suck them in tightly as if puckering up to give a kiss. This may draw the perpetrator's fingers inward, toward the teeth, perhaps within biting distance.

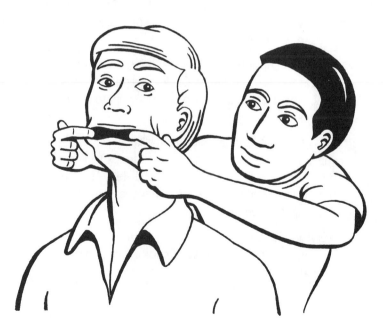

FART CUP

PAIN	ANNOYANCE	EMBARRASSMENT	DIFFICULTY	TOTAL POINTS OUT OF 40
2	8	5	7	22

DEFINITION

Fart Cup (*färt kup*): Expelling gas into one's cupped hand, then quickly placing the hand in close proximity to a person's face and uncapping, so as to release the odor.

TIPS FOR EXECUTION

☞ Like its cousins the Burp 'n' Blow, the "Pull My Finger," and the Dutch Oven, menu foresight is the fart cupper's best ally; fill up on burritos, chili, or other bean-laden foods in preparation.

☞ The victim should be no farther than three feet away at the time of the fart; odor scienticians have demonstrated that smell waves will dissipate at greater distances.

☞ Avoid the Fart Cup in cold weather environments where gloves are worn, as the smell tends to linger in the fabric at the point of attempted release (a simple rule of thumb: "If you're wearing a glove, show the Fart Cup no love").

☞ Beginning cuppers will typically employ silent-but-deadlies as the ammunition of choice. As confidence and experience grows, just rip and grip.

FART CUP

POSSIBLE COUNTERMEASURES

☞ Use a shirt collar, turtleneck, or sweatshirt hood to provide a garbed defense. Note: this raises the odds of a Hoodwink, however.

☞ Should wardrobe circumstances not allow the above, try to grab the perpetrator's outstretched arm and execute a Native American Burn.

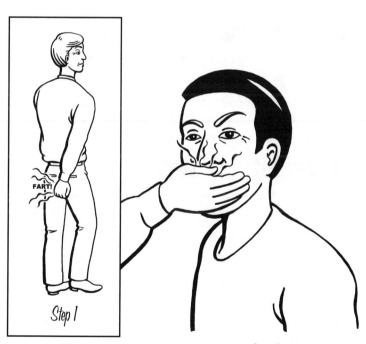

FART!

Step 1

Step 2

FISP

PAIN	ANNOYANCE	EMBARRASSMENT	DIFFICULTY	TOTAL POINTS OUT OF 40
2	2	4	2	10

DEFINITION

FISP ('fisp): Abbreviated form of finger in someone's personage; the action of extending one's index finger level to a person's face in profile, followed by calling that person's attention so as to draw the turning face into the extended finger.

TIPS FOR EXECUTION

☞ Stay out of the victim's field of vision by standing both to the side and to the slight rear.

☞ Utter phrases such as, "Oh my God!," "That girl is hot!," or "Look—Aurora Borealis!" to increase the likelihood that the victim will turn quickly.

POSSIBLE COUNTERMEASURES

☞ Note that the FISP is difficult to avoid, as it is the natural tendency to turn when one's attention is drawn.

☞ Slowly turn whenever called, lessening the impact of possible FISPs.

☞ Lift a hand to the side of the face to serve as a shield whenever turning.

☞ Improve peripheral vision to better survey the area for possible extended fingers.

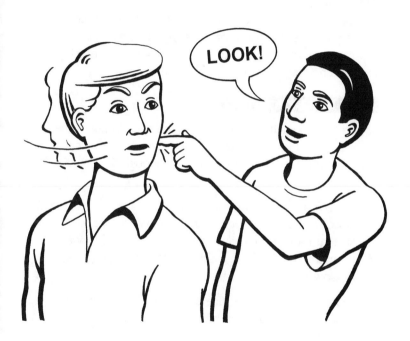

FLAT FOOT

PAIN	ANNOYANCE	EMBARRASSMENT	DIFFICULTY	TOTAL POINTS OUT OF 40
2	8	8	6	24

DEFINITION

Flat Foot (*flat fut*): The act of stepping on the back edge of a person's shoe while that person is in motion, thereby causing the heel to lift out of the shoe completely and the top rear edge of the shoe to curl underneath the newly exposed heel; also known as a Flat Tire.

TIPS FOR EXECUTION

☞ Striking the actual shoe and not the sock or leg of the victim is of key importance. Striking the leg will alert the victim and will usually provide enough time to avoid the flat.

☞ A perfect strike hits the very bottom edge of the shoe, close to the sole, directly before the victim intends to lift that foot. In such cases, the victim's natural forward momentum will lift the heel out of its housing (a.k.a. A Blowout).

☞ Optimal conditions include situations where authority figures such as teachers, camp counselors, or wardens are requiring a single-file line-up.

Execution

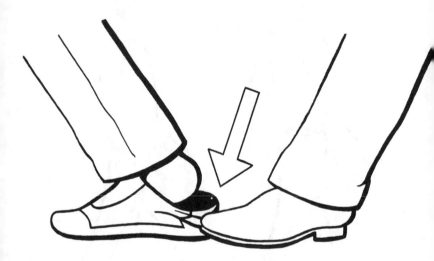

Detail

FLAT FOOT

☞ Go barefoot.

☞ In the event that footwear is unavoidable, select shoes with laces, and tie them as tightly as good circulation will allow.

☞ The perpetrator often requires several attempts to score a flat. If a suspected unsuccessful attempt is felt along the back of the heel, begin running or zigzagging to deter future attempts. Alternatively, stop walking immediately so that the perpetrator is forced into a collision.

☞ In the event that damage is sustained, wiggle the foot in question from side-to-side to attempt reinsertion.

☞ In the event that the side-to-side method of reinsertion fails, a full stop may be required so that the shoe can be totally removed and replaced. Note: this will likely cause extreme embarrassment.

FLOUR SHOWER

PAIN	ANNOYANCE	EMBARRASSMENT	DIFFICULTY	TOTAL POINTS OUT OF 40
2	10	4	9	25

DEFINITION

Flour Shower (*flour shaur*): Pouring flour on someone in the midst of a shower, so as to cause a sticky paste to form.

TIPS FOR EXECUTION

☞ The Flour Shower is among the most difficult acts of roguery to execute, as the flour-to-water ratio must be absolutely perfect.

☞ A Flour Shower with too little flour will allow the victim to simply rinse off the powder. Too much flour, however, will cause clumping.

☞ The goal of the Flour Shower is a coating of approximately a quarter-inch (.64 centimeters) across a wide swath of the victim's body.

☞ Current United States plumbing regulations recommend a PSI (pounds per square inch) in the 45 to 50 range, with a flow of 2.5 gallons per minute; using this as a guideline, it is essential to pour between 3 and 3.5 cups of flour on the victim.

☞ Water flow may vary by region, so check with local municipal water district officials before executing.

FLOUR SHOWER

☞ Like the Polar Shower, a secure perimeter is the best defense; if the perpetrator can't enter the bathroom (or the pantry, for that matter), the Flour Shower has no chance of success.

☞ If an imminent Flour Shower attack is detected, grab the shower head, step out of its spray, turn the shower temperature to its coldest setting, and use it to douse the assailant. Note: this is also effective against the Polar Shower.

☞ If you are the victim of the Flour Shower, make the best of the situation; scrape off the sticky mess and use it to finish any lingering art or masonry projects.

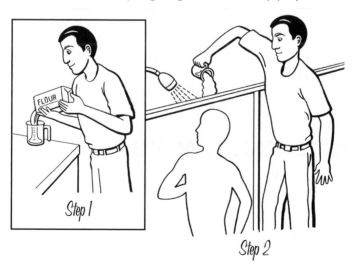

Step 1

Step 2

HEAD BUTT

PAIN	ANNOYANCE	EMBARRASSMENT	DIFFICULTY	TOTAL POINTS OUT OF 40
10	9	6	9	34

DEFINITION

Head Butt (*hed butt*): The act of smashing one's forehead into another person's face, head, or nose in a forceful downward motion.

TIPS FOR EXECUTION

☞ Proximity to the victim is essential; the long-distance Head Butt (beyond one foot away from the victim) has little chance of success.

☞ Sneezes and coughs share the some motion as the Head Butt; faking such a bodily function may aid the successful execution.

☞ Under all circumstances keep a clenched jaw during this maneuver to prevent chipping a tooth (and other general tooth trauma).

☞ Choose a target of equal or shorter height; the "jumping" or "tiptoe" Head Butt is rarely successful.

POSSIBLE COUNTERMEASURES

☞ Beware of people who speak softly to draw people close to them as they talk; this is perfect cover for the Head Butt.

HEAD BUTT

☞ When speaking to someone face-to-face, shift body angles and positions periodically to create a moving target; remember to vary the tempo of each cycle so the perpetrator cannot time his move.

☞ While popular fashion tends to vary, a strong knit wool cap should provide both essential padding and an element of style to a person's wardrobe.

HERTZ DONUT

PAIN	ANNOYANCE	EMBARRASSMENT	DIFFICULTY	TOTAL POINTS OUT OF 40
8	8	6	7	29

DEFINITION

Hertz Donut (*hurts dOnut*): Asking a person if he or she would like a "hertz donut" and, upon an affirmative reply, punching said person in the arm while asking, "Hurts, don't it?"

TIPS FOR EXECUTION

☞ The Hertz Donut is difficult to execute against anyone who has previously felt the tantalizing promise of a tasty pastry give way to the bitter sting of a sucker punch.

☞ It may help to sell the unsuspecting victim by pretending to have just finished one's own delicious hertz donut; in this regard, a dab of powdered sugar on the chin is a powerful ally.

The Set-Up

☞ Carry a bag or other container that could plausibly be used to contain the donut in question.

☞ Display some degree of reluctance to part with the imaginary donut; begging for the hertz donut will make the victim feel doubly stupid upon its delivery.

POSSIBLE COUNTERMEASURES

☞ Ask to see the offered donut before deciding whether to accept it, but make sure to take a step back before doing so (as the perpetrator may mistake this reply for a "yes").

☞ Ask what flavor the donut is, where it came from, and other questions that may flush the unprepared assailant out.

☞ A low-carb diet should help one avoid donuts of any type.

The Pay-Off

HOODWINK

PAIN	ANNOYANCE	EMBARRASSMENT	DIFFICULTY	TOTAL POINTS OUT OF 40
2	9	9	7	27

DEFINITION

Hoodwink (*hudwingk*): The act of pulling the drawstrings of a hooded sweatshirt so that the hood closes around the face of the victim and renders him temporarily blind.

TIPS FOR EXECUTION

☞ Best times to strike are when the victim is sitting down doing warm-up exercises or watching TV on the sofa.

☞ Approach the victim from behind; remember, the victim's side vision is mostly obscured by the hood, so take some time in locating the drawstrings.

☞ Pull the strings tight in one clean, swift jerk.

☞ Team up with accomplices to combine the Hoodwink with other acts of roguery such as the Noogie, the Atomic Wedgie, or the Pink Belly; the more simultaneous attacks executed while the victim is blinded, the better.

☞ After a successful attack, try tying the drawstrings together in a knot to make it more difficult for the victim to remove his hood (Permanent Midnight).

☞ Stick with attacks on hooded victims until the technique is mastered; while it is possible to strike a person whose hood is in the down position, the added effort of raising the hood and pulling both drawstrings in rapid succession increases the risk of failure.

HOODWINK

☞ Choose snug, non-knitted stocking caps in lieu of hoods for morning workouts, and always face workout buddies and running mates on cold days.

☞ If wearing a hooded sweatshirt is mandatory (as in some cults), keep the hood in the down position whenever possible.

☞ Cut the drawstrings to the minimum length possible to reduce the surface area of a potential attack.

☞ Never doze off with a hooded sweatshirt in the up position; in addition to the Hoodwink, this is a prime opportunity for a Charley Horse, Magic Mustache, Pink Belly, Shoe Tie, or Warm Water Manicure.

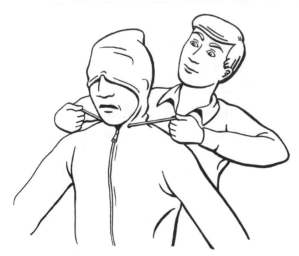

ICY

PAIN	ANNOYANCE	EMBARRASSMENT	DIFFICULTY	TOTAL POINTS OUT OF 40
5	9	8	6	28

DEFINITION

Icy (*is-E*): Pulling back a person's shirt or pants, typically from behind, and dumping a quantity of ice or snow between the victim's skin and clothes.

TIPS FOR EXECUTION

☞ The Icy is best executed in winter for two reasons: snow and slush in colder climates provide an abundance of ammunition, and a summer Icy is often viewed as a refreshing gesture of kindness.

☞ Quick execution is key; fumbling to create a window between the victim's clothes and skin may cause the snow or ice to melt.

☞ Seek out victims either just returning from or just preparing to go outside; this provides close access to the door should a quick escape be needed.

POSSIBLE COUNTERMEASURES

☞ A hooded sweatshirt, drawstring pants, or other tightly bound clothing will make execution of the Icy very difficult; however, this does leave open the possibility of the Hoodwink.

ICY

☞ Be wary of pats on the back, hair tussles, or any other action that places the potential perpetrator's hands in the Icy "hot zone."

☞ If repeated Icy attacks occur, consider relocation to Florida, Arizona, or other temperate climates.

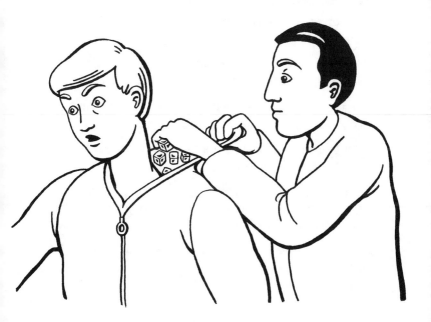

"KICK ME" SIGN

PAIN	ANNOYANCE	EMBARRASSMENT	DIFFICULTY	TOTAL POINTS OUT OF 40
7	5	10	4	26

DEFINITION

"Kick Me" Sign (*kik mE sIn*): The art of taping a provocative message to a victim's back, especially a message urging the general public to harm the unwitting sign bearer.

TIPS FOR EXECUTION

☞ It is essential to attach the sign without the victim's knowledge.

☞ A firm, friendly pat on the back or an "accidental" collision can provide good pretexts for contact.

☞ Employ the stickiest tape possible, as the jarring motion of walking is apt to knock the sign loose.

☞ Write in large, capital letters, as poor penmanship can render the effect of the sign useless.

☞ For a traditional "Kick Me" Sign, the best results are achieved when a large arrow pointing down toward the victim's butt is included.

☞ Entice as many people as possible (especially class or office bullies) to take action by bringing the sign to their attention.

"KICK ME" SIGN

POSSIBLE COUNTERMEASURES

☞ Check for the presence of a sign every time someone pats the back, especially if the pat comes from an enemy or a casual acquaintance about whom little is known.

☞ If kicked in the butt, immediately run hands across the back to check for new postings.

☞ Wear fleece, wool, or other materials to which tape does not adhere.

☞ Be on the lookout for this in any type of line formation situation: lines for the DMV, school assemblies, and return from recess are moments of extreme vulnerability.

KNEE BEND

PAIN	ANNOYANCE	EMBARRASSMENT	DIFFICULTY	TOTAL POINTS OUT OF 40
2	6	5	4	17

DEFINITION

Knee Bend (*nE bend*): The act of jabbing a knee into the back of a standing person's fully extended leg in such a manner as to cause that person to lose balance and fall.

TIPS FOR EXECUTION

☞ Search out motionless victims who are leaning heavily against one leg.

☞ Always attack the straightest leg as that is the one apt to be bearing the most weight. Note that peg-legged pirates are the obvious exception to this rule.

☞ Aim squarely for the back of the knee; if the victim turns around during the attack, consider landing the strike on the thigh for a modified Charley Horse.

☞ The best people to strike include those who are either tired or distracted by another activity (e.g., those waiting in line, drinking, or singing in a chorus concert).

POSSIBLE COUNTERMEASURES

☞ Enroll in a Tai Chi class to improve balance.

☞ Whenever possible, use at least one arm to prop up body weight and provide extra shock absorption. When drinking a glass of water, for instance, lean against a counter.

KNEE BEND

☞In general, avoid standing in long lines. In addition to Knee Bends, lines are breeding grounds for the Flat Foot, "Kick Me" Sign, Mosquito Flick, Pants Yank, Rat Tail, Shoulder Tap, Atomic Wedgie, and a whole host of other rogueries. Call ahead to make an appointment, arrive during off-peak hours, or send a delegate to avoid lines.

KNUCKLE MASH

PAIN	ANNOYANCE	EMBARRASSMENT	DIFFICULTY	TOTAL POINTS OUT OF 40
9	9	3	9	30

DEFINITION

Knuckle Mash (*nu-kul mash*): The result of placing one's hand on top of another's, curling both sets of fingers inward until a tight fist is formed by the bottom hand, and squeezing hard enough to cause intense pain to the victim's knuckles.

TIPS FOR EXECUTION

☞ Remember three letters—T.O.T. (Tips-on-Tips); once the victim's fingers are controlled, dig around until the very tips of his fingers are enveloped.

☞ Pull inward and upward as hard as possible; picture the victim's middle knuckle kissing the dead center of the palm.

☞ Numerous studies show that rapid oscillations between pain and relief intensify pain levels considerably. Add some zip with the Swedish pulsing technique: 1) squeeze hard. 2) release momentarily. 3) repeat. Suggested pulse rate is one to two times per second for 10 seconds or as long as circumstances permit.

KNUCKLE MASH

POSSIBLE COUNTERMEASURES

☞ Keep fingernails long, as this makes it difficult for the perpetrator to get Tips-On-Tips.

☞ Tension balls and other grip strengtheners can help build hand and finger muscles; amaze and scare the perpetrator by breaking the Knuckle Mash grip with a single well-timed finger flex.

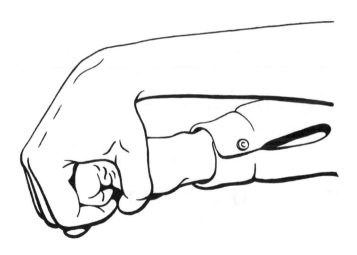

LIFT LIES

PAIN	ANNOYANCE	EMBARRASSMENT	DIFFICULTY	TOTAL POINTS OUT OF 40
1	7	8	4	20

DEFINITION

Lift Lies (*lift lîs*): Engaging in a particularly embarrassing or uncomfortable discussion while in an elevator, to the chagrin, embarrassment, and/or annoyance of other passengers.

TIPS FOR EXECUTION

☞ Medical conditions, intimate encounters, or outrageous exploits make the best Lift Lies; they tantalize and repulse the audience simultaneously.

☞ Inappropriate remarks may be self-directed ("So the doctor told me to drain it twice a week and be careful how I sit.") or focused on a co-conspirator ("Is it still yellow or has it finally turned clear?").

☞ A successful Lift Liar has never gone wrong using the following three terms: "pus," "negligee," and "parole violation."

POSSIBLE COUNTERMEASURES

☞ Join in on the fun by sharing one's own (presumably fictitious) stories related to the perpetrator's tale ("I had a sore like that once, too!").

☞ Deflate the situation by pretending to not speak English. Note: this technique is rendered more effective by mastering a dozen or so words in a foreign language.

☞ In desperate situations, press the emergency exit button and climb or rappel to the nearest floor.

LIGHT FLICK

PAIN	ANNOYANCE	EMBARRASSMENT	DIFFICULTY	TOTAL POINTS OUT OF 40
1	5	3	1	10

DEFINITION

Light Flick (*līt flik*): Turning the light off and on while a person is using the bathroom, so as to cause disorientation and annoyance.

TIPS FOR EXECUTION

☞ The ideal bathroom is one that has its light switch placed on the outside of the door so that the perpetrator has easy access and the victim does not.

☞ There are two basic categories of victim: 1) showerers. 2) those using the toilet (the aptly named "Category Number Two's").

☞ The best Light Flick is one with randomly timed intervals. By waiting long periods between flicks, the victim will be lulled into a false belief that the attack has passed.

☞ If executing a Light Flick from inside the bathroom, make sure to keep your eyes closed to prevent dizziness or nausea.

☞ For an aggressive execution, follow up with a Polar Shower or Flour Shower.

LIGHT FLICK

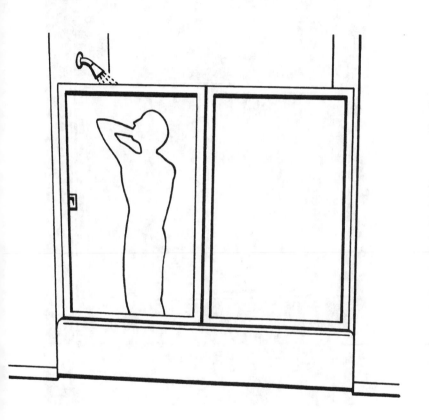

Step 1 ⟹

Step 2

LIGHT FLICK

POSSIBLE COUNTERMEASURES

☞ Seek out bathrooms with light switches on the inside and locking doors. Such a setup makes the Light Flick virtually impossible for all but the wiliest assailants.

☞ If you are the victim of a Light Flick while showering, immediately drop to the stall floor and curl into the fetal position, as a low center of gravity should lower the risk of disorientation.

☞ For Category Number Two Light Flicks, it may be necessary to simply grab hold of something stable (the vanity, the toilet tank, etc.) and ride it out.

☞ In areas of extreme high risk, consider "holding it" until a safer bathroom situation can be secured.

LOOSE LID

PAIN	ANNOYANCE	EMBARRASSMENT	DIFFICULTY	TOTAL POINTS OUT OF 40
2	5	5	2	14

DEFINITION

Loose Lid (*lüs lid*): Loosening the cap of a salt or pepper shaker so that the entire contents spill out the next time a person uses it.

TIPS FOR EXECUTION

☞ The victim's attention must be diverted for the shaker lid to be successfully prepared.

☞ Forethought bears dividends; loosen the cap before the victim reaches the dining area.

☞ For "seasoned" perpetrators, try upping the ante by loosening both the salt and pepper lids; the victim may flush out the first attempt, but he is not likely to expect The Double Loose Lid.

POSSIBLE COUNTERMEASURES

☞ Pre-check all shaker lids before using.

☞ Eat pre-spiced foods.

☞ Switch to a low sodium diet.

☞ Come prepared: carry individual salt and pepper packets at all times.

MAGIC MUSTACHE

PAIN	ANNOYANCE	EMBARRASSMENT	DIFFICULTY	TOTAL POINTS OUT OF 40
1	9	10	10	30

DEFINITION

Magic Mustache (*ma-jik mus-'stash*): Drawing facial hair in magic marker on a sleeping victim's face.

TIPS FOR EXECUTION

☞ The time and obtrusiveness necessary to complete the Magic Mustache render successful execution very difficult. As a result, select victims based on their deep sleeping ability or level of intoxication.

☞ Use a non-scented marker; the proximity of the mustache area to the nose raises the possibility that an odorous pen might wake the victim.

☞ Get creative: try a Van Dyke, soul patch, or even mutton chops.

POSSIBLE COUNTERMEASURES

☞ If possible, secure the sleeping area by locking the door.

☞ In a high-risk situation, set a trip wire close to the bed so that perpetrator will be unable to sneak attack.

☞ Grow an actual mustache to remove the palette of opportunity.

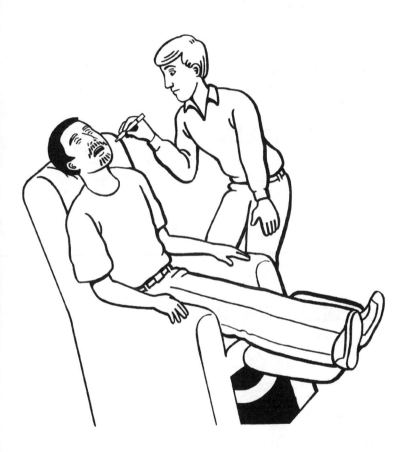

MARKER SNIFF

PAIN	ANNOYANCE	EMBARRASSMENT	DIFFICULTY	TOTAL POINTS OUT OF 40
2	8	7	2	19

DEFINITION

Marker Sniff (*mär-kur snif*): Convincing a person that a magic marker has an interesting aroma, so that the victim exposes his nose to verify and is written upon.

TIPS FOR EXECUTION

☞ A marker with a strong scent is an ideal weapon, as the victim will be able to pick up a hint of the smell before leaning in for the full sniff.

☞ Dark colored markers will leave a more obvious mark than light colored ones.

☞ For a particularly embarrassing (and long-lasting) Marker Sniff, employ an indelible ink marker.

POSSIBLE COUNTERMEASURES

☞ Do not attempt to sniff any object that might leave a mark on the nose.

☞ If curiosity outweighs caution, take possession of the marker before sniffing it, then step beyond arms' reach before bringing close to the nose.

☞ Carry wet-naps or rubbing alcohol and cotton swabs at all times as an emergency Marker Sniff removal kit.

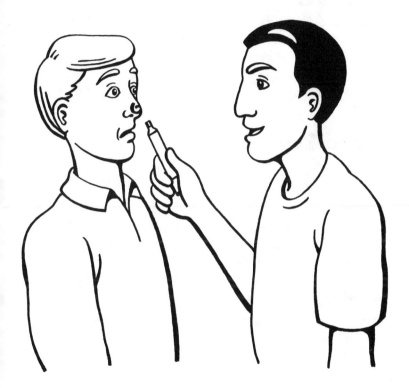

MOSQUITO FLICK

PAIN	ANNOYANCE	EMBARRASSMENT	DIFFICULTY	TOTAL POINTS OUT OF 40
2	9	6	4	21

DEFINITION

Mosquito Flick (*mu-'skE-tO flik*): Brushing a person lightly with a stick or other object, typically near the ear or back of the neck, in a manner leading the person to believe that a mosquito is the cause of irritation; note that the Mosquito Flick is similar in execution and annoyance to the Shoulder Tap.

TIPS FOR EXECUTION

☞ Use a soft-tipped object such as a long blade of wild grass or a pussy willow to better simulate the feel of a mosquito.

☞ The Mosquito Flick utensil should be between 14 and 18 inches long. If it is any shorter, the perpetrator will lack the distance necessary for a plausible deniability; if it is any longer, the utensil will be too unwieldy to effectively control.

☞ To heighten irritation, perform the Mosquito Flick repeatedly, at varying intervals and on different body parts.

MOSQUITO FLICK

POSSIBLE COUNTERMEASURES

☞ A foolproof but impractical defense against the Mosquito Flick is to wear insect repellent at all times.

☞ Listen carefully for the buzz of the insect; if none is present, assume the Mosquito Flick is being executed.

☞ If the Mosquito Flick is suspected, relocate so that the assailant cannot repeat the procedure.

☞ Turn quickly and attempt to catch the perpetrator in the act. Note: the Mosquito Flick-to-FISP combination, though rare, is a possibility.

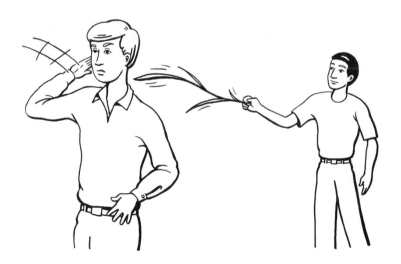

NATIVE AMERICAN BURN

PAIN	ANNOYANCE	EMBARRASSMENT	DIFFICULTY	TOTAL POINTS OUT OF 40
9	8	5	5	27

DEFINITION

Native American Burn (*nA-tiv amer-a-ken bern*):
A burning, itching sensation created on the forearm when a person grabs hold of another's bare arm and simultaneously wrings both palms in opposite directions; note that all successful Native American burns involve changing the color of the affected skin to a bright red hue; formerly known as Indian Burn.

TIPS FOR EXECUTION

☞ The degree of Native American Burn is directly proportional to the amount of friction applied to the forearm.

☞ To maximize friction, ensure that both palms and the victim's arm are totally dry; oily, sweaty, or otherwise wet surfaces on either person will cause the grip to slide and lessen the degree of pain and color change.

☞ Native American Burns done on top of clothing do not tend to be effective, so ensure that the victim is short-sleeved and/or naked.

☞ For advanced execution, attempt to ensnare as much of the victim's forearm hair as possible; the hair will pull the skin and will end up in micro-knots that will be difficult or impossible for the victim to untie after the attack is complete.

NATIVE AMERICAN BURN

☞ Wear long sleeves whenever possible.

☞ If you are under attack, employ the hand of the non-affected arm to remove the perpetrator's grip. This can be done by clasping the perpetrator's fingertips on one hand, and pulling back. For a truly aggressive defense, turn this move into a Knuckle Mash.

☞ Sunscreen is an effective defense against both melanoma and the Native American Burn; apply liberally.

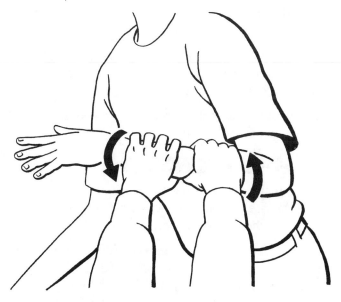

NOOGIE

PAIN	ANNOYANCE	EMBARRASSMENT	DIFFICULTY	TOTAL POINTS OUT OF 40
10	10	9	8	37

DEFINITION

Noogie (*nu-g*E): The act of drilling one's knuckle(s) into a person's head using a rapid lateral scraping and twisting motion.

TIPS FOR EXECUTION

☞ Employ a headlock to immobilize the victim throughout the attack.

☞ For taller targets, wait until the victim is either seated or hunched over (e.g., tying shoes).

☞ Similar to Native American Burns, it is important to twist and pull as much hair into the process as possible to increase the pain level.

☞ Try shouting "Nooooooooooooogieeeeeeeee!" the entire time for added effect.

POSSIBLE COUNTERMEASURES

☞ A common first reaction is to try to wiggle free; as this only increases the movement of the head and intensifies the pain, try to keep relatively still.

☞ Use the chin to dig into the assailant's chest as much as possible; if you are often the victim of a Serial Noogier (e.g., older brother), strengthen the chin through practice by drilling into large throw pillows.

☞As with the Head Butt, a sturdy wool cap provides a simple and fashionable defense against the Noogie.

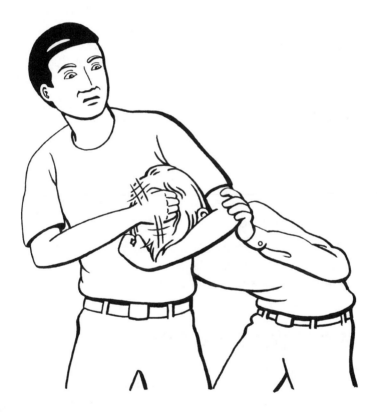

NOSE TWEAK

PAIN	ANNOYANCE	EMBARRASSMENT	DIFFICULTY	TOTAL POINTS OUT OF 40
4	6	6	2	18

DEFINITION

Nose Tweak (*nOz twEk*): The act of pointing to a person's shirt, inquiring about some fictitious spot on it, waiting for the victim to look down, and then raising the index finger into the base of the victim's nose; also known as "what's that on your shirt?"

TIPS FOR EXECUTION

☞ Utter earnestness and conviction will sell the act; try to actually envision a spot or stain on the target's shirt.

☞ Squint as if really trying to see something interesting.

☞ Move the index finger slowly toward the victim's shirt as if afraid to touch something so nasty.

☞ Aim for a spot high on the shirt, close to victim's neck. This will minimize the distance between the finger and the nose and lessen execution time.

☞ To rub it in, say "Gotcha!" after a successful strike.

POSSIBLE COUNTERMEASURES

☞ If someone points out a spot or stain, step backward before looking down to investigate; this should create enough distance from the perpetrator to avoid a connection.

☞ Another approach is simply to avoid looking down at all costs; there will be plenty of time to check out the shirt later, once the coast is clear.

☞ If a strike is obvious, grab the assailant's finger with either hand and bend backward; this may deter future attempts.

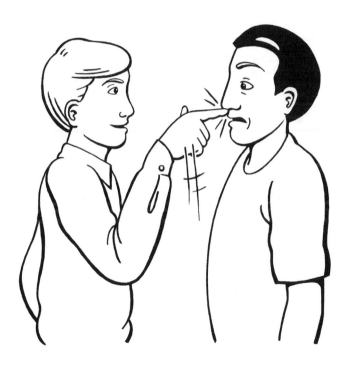

OTTOMAN

PAIN	ANNOYANCE	EMBARRASSMENT	DIFFICULTY	TOTAL POINTS OUT OF 40
8	10	9	3	30

DEFINITION

Ottoman (*ät-tO-man*): The act of toppling a standing person backward over a footstool or kneeling person.

TIPS FOR EXECUTION

☞ Engage the target in small talk while setting up the maneuver; just prior to striking, lean in close, well past normal conversational comfort boundaries, so that the victim will step backward.

☞ Once the victim has moved into place (above the accomplice or footstool), complete the Ottoman with a quick double strike to the pectoral region using both palms open and outstretched.

☞ The kneeling accomplice should crouch into a tight ball and should get as close as possible to the back of the victim's calves. Note: arching the back too high or setting up too far away gives the person a chance to break or prevent the fall.

☞ Choose an uncluttered grassy or carpeted landing zone for the victim. An Ottoman on hardwood floors, marble, or travertine tile may result in severe injury.

OTTOMAN

POSSIBLE COUNTERMEASURES

☞ Remove all freestanding footstools from the house; Lay-Z-Boy recliners with lever-controlled footrests provide a safe—and comfortable—alternative.

☞ When you are conversing with someone face-to-face, lean in somewhat toward the speaker to provide a signal of interest (genuine or feigned) while foiling the Ottoman at the same time.

☞ If you are pushed over an accomplice, remain calm; as with most falls, tensing up prior to impact may exacerbate injuries.

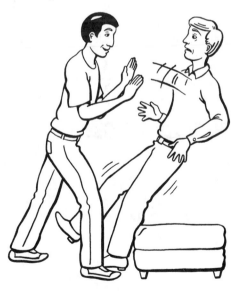

PACE MATCH

PAIN	ANNOYANCE	EMBARRASSMENT	DIFFICULTY	TOTAL POINTS OUT OF 40
1	7	5	8	21

DEFINITION

Pace Match (*'pAs mach*): Walking in very close proximity to, and at matching pace with, another person while appearing oblivious to that person's presence; note that the Pace Match is successfully executed only if the pace is continuously adjusted in response to the person's change in walking speed.

TIPS FOR EXECUTION

☞ Carry a newspaper, engage in a cell phone discussion, or provide some other form of camouflage so that the matching of pace appears, to the victim, to be unintentional.

☞ Remain at least an arm's length from the victim to avoid collision in the event of a sudden stop.

POSSIBLE COUNTERMEASURES

☞ Stop walking so that there is no pace to match.

☞ Should stopping not be possible (e.g., hurrying through an airport to catch a plane), continuously alter the pace or move in a zigzagging or serpentine motion to wear down the assailant's resolve.

PACE MATCH

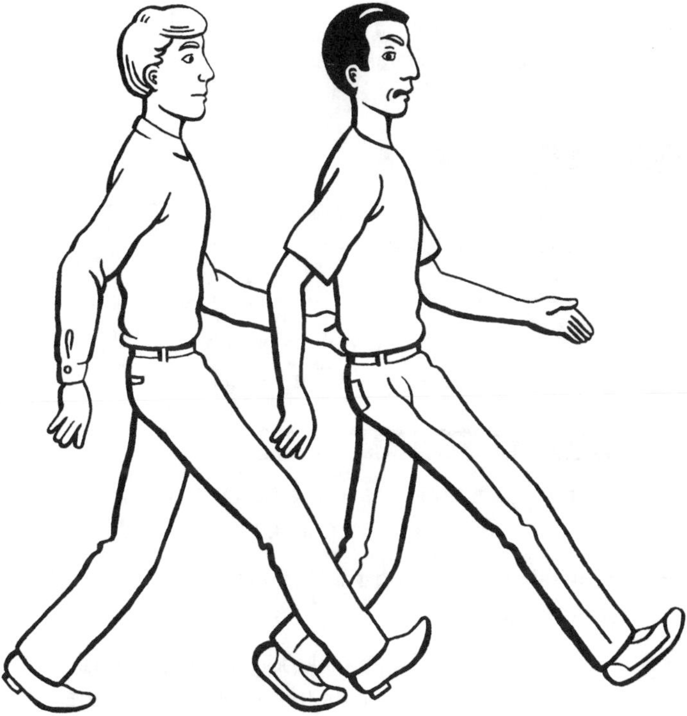

PANTS YANK

PAIN	ANNOYANCE	EMBARRASSMENT	DIFFICULTY	TOTAL POINTS OUT OF 40
2	10	10	4	26

DEFINITION

Pants Yank (*'pants ya[ng]k*): The action of grabbing a person's pants at the waist and yanking downward toward the ankles.

TIPS FOR EXECUTION

☞ A rear approach is typically most effective, enhancing the element of surprise.

☞ Seek out victims with loose-fitting clothing.

☞ For aggressive execution, seek to grab hold of the victim's underpants as well (The Revealer).

POSSIBLE COUNTERMEASURES

☞ Make intelligent clothing and accessory choices, such as belts, button flies, and tight-fitting pants.

☞ For assaults from behind, see Atomic Wedgie countermeasures.

☞ Remember that the Pants Yank does happen in real life; as such, avoid undergarments that might deepen the embarrassment of the yank (e.g., Underoos, and granny panties).

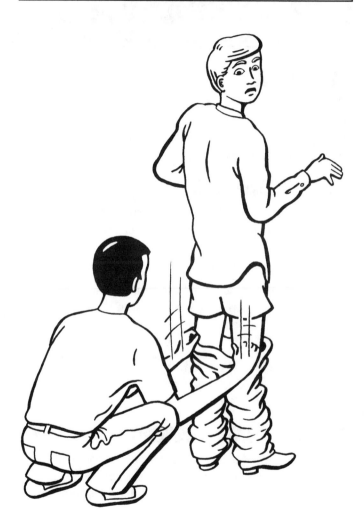

PILLOW MINT

PAIN	ANNOYANCE	EMBARRASSMENT	DIFFICULTY	TOTAL POINTS OUT OF 40
3	8	6	4	21

DEFINITION

Pillow Mint (*pi-lO mint*): Dabbing a sleeping person's pillow with shaving cream, toothpaste, or other sticky substances so that when rolling over during the night the victim's face gets covered in the goo.

TIPS FOR EXECUTION

☞ While the name Pillow Mint would indicate a scented substance is required, this is a dangerous misnomer; pungent odors may be difficult to apply on all but the most congested victims.

☞ Ideally, seek out victims whose heads are in the middle of the pillow. By placing substances on both edges of the pillow, the odds of successful execution are doubled. This is known as The Oreo.

☞ Shaving cream cans tend to be quite noisy, so dispense the foam onto one's hand or applicator device at a safe distance from the victim.

POSSIBLE COUNTERMEASURES

☞ Tucking oneself under the covers in a cocoon-like fashion should prevent the Pillow Mint; however, it dramatically increases the odds of a self-inflicted Dutch Oven.

PILLOW MINT

☞ Place mousetraps on either side of the pillow. Note: this may cause severe injury to one's own ears (The Tyson).

☞ Practice the ancient yoga pose of Advasana, which places the body stomach-down and the arms lifted to the sides of the head, until it becomes second nature. Sleeping in this position provides an impenetrable defense.

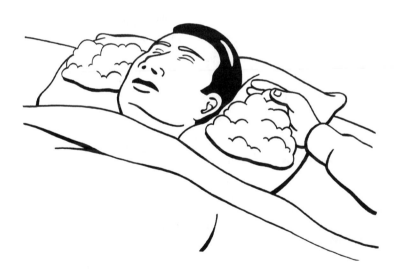

PINK BELLY

PAIN	ANNOYANCE	EMBARRASSMENT	DIFFICULTY	TOTAL POINTS OUT OF 40
9	9	8	7	33

DEFINITION

Pink Belly (*pi[ng]k be-lE*): The flat-palmed slapping or tapping of a person's stomach, so as to leave a pink or red mark.

TIPS FOR EXECUTION

☞ Bare stomach skin is a necessity; seek out victims at pool parties, locker rooms, or fashion shows.

☞ Keep palms completely flat, as cupping the hand mutes both the force and sound of the slap.

☞ Take a long swing to build up momentum and speed, but just prior to impact on the belly, pull back sharply on the downward motion. This creates more of a whipping effect and should enhance the resulting welt.

☞ A perfect strike should leave a full imprint of the palm; strive to leave a "signature" in every execution.

☞ Seated people make poor targets, as their folded belly skin will diffuse the impact and sound.

POSSIBLE COUNTERMEASURES

☞ Avoid teenybopper fashion trends that bare the navel; wear T-shirts whenever possible and tuck them deeply into pants.

PINK BELLY

☞ If a perpetrator is poised mid-strike and impact cannot be avoided, suck in the gut immediately; this alters the surface area and can lessen the blow's impact.

☞ Sleep on the stomach or in the fetal position to reduce exposure to night attacks.

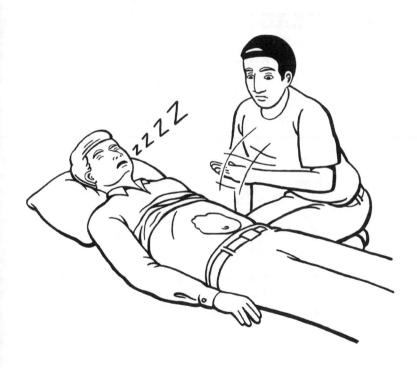

POLAR SHOWER

PAIN	ANNOYANCE	EMBARRASSMENT	DIFFICULTY	TOTAL POINTS OUT OF 40
5	9	4	4	22

DEFINITION

Polar Shower (*pO-ler shaur*): Pouring a cup or pitcher of ice-cold water on someone in the midst of a warm or hot shower.

TIPS FOR EXECUTION

☞ There are two primary techniques one may employ to douse the victim in cold water: 1) over the curtain or stall door (The Niagara). 2) opening the curtain or stall door (The Norman Bates).

☞ It is of critical importance to actually hit the victim with the cold water; a miss will scare the prey but also embarrass the assailant.

☞ To increase the likelihood of a successful payload delivery, remember to use a big container and to dump the contents over a wide geographic area; it is unlikely that the victim can hide in one corner of the shower and foil such a technique.

☞ Scouting out the potential victim's showering habits to plan for successful execution has some upside, but it may look odd if discovered by either the victim or a third party.

POLAR SHOWER

☞ If at all possible, lock the bathroom door. A secure perimeter renders the polar shower impossible; this will also defend against the Flour Shower.

☞ Many plumbing systems are sensitive to increased system loads; in other words, a change in shower pressure may indicate that someone is preparing artillery for an assault.

☞ If an imminent polar shower attack is detected, grab the showerhead, step out of its spray, turn the shower temperature to its coldest setting, and use it to douse the assailant. Note: this is also effective against the Flour Shower.

PSYCHE SHAKE

PAIN	ANNOYANCE	EMBARRASSMENT	DIFFICULTY	TOTAL POINTS OUT OF 40
1	5	6	1	13

DEFINITION

Psyche Shake (*slk shAk*): Extending one's hand as if to shake the victim's hand, only to withdraw the offer at the last moment while shouting, "Psyche!"

TIPS FOR EXECUTION

☞ The Psyche Shake should be executed upon first encountering the victim; an attempted handshake in the middle of a conversation or activity is bound to raise suspicion.

☞ Employing the Psyche Shake on new acquaintances will increase the likelihood of success, but decrease the chance of enduring friendship.

☞ Younger perpetrators, or hipper adults, may wish to try the close cousin of the Psyche Shake—The Psyche High Five (remember the mantra, "give me five/up high/down low/too slow" for the classic Four Step Variation).

☞ To add a useful layer of grooming to the act, complete the Psyche Shake by using the formerly extended hand to comb through one's hair.

The Set-Up

The Pay-Off

PSYCHE SHAKE

POSSIBLE COUNTERMEASURES

☞ Grasp the prospective assailant's bait hand with one's own secondary hand before accepting the shake with the primary hand; this is known as the All-State Defense.

☞ When suspicious of a possible impending Psyche Shake, fake a sneeze into one's own hand before offering it.

☞ Employ the Asian method of bowing in lieu of a traditional Western handshake.

"PULL MY FINGER"

PAIN	ANNOYANCE	EMBARRASSMENT	DIFFICULTY	TOTAL POINTS OUT OF 40
1	3	4	7	15

DEFINITION

"Pull My Finger" (*pul ml fi[ng]-ger*): Asking a person to grasp and tug one's index finger and then expelling gas immediately afterward.

TIPS FOR EXECUTION

☞ Timing is imperative for the successful "Pull My Finger" execution; farting too early (Premature Expilation) or too late (Premature Fingulation) will cause major embarrassment for the perpetrator.

☞ Beans, Mexican entrees, and Hormel products should facilitate the stomach distress necessary for gas build-up.

☞ Like the Hertz Donut, it is difficult to execute the "Pull My Finger" on anyone who has fallen prey to a prior pungent pull; search for victims among the young, the curious, the Amish, or the foreign exchange crowd.

☞ Silent-but-deadlies leave open the possibility of blaming the odor on the victim; this will up the embarrassment factor to a perfect 10.

POSSIBLE COUNTERMEASURES

☞ As a general rule, be very wary whenever someone requests a pull of any of his body parts.

"PULL MY FINGER"

☞ Stalling or delaying the pull may cause the perpetrator to expel the gas prematurely.

☞ Play along, but immediately after pulling, yank the perpetrator's shirt or polar fleece over his head to create a modified Dutch Oven.

PURPLE NURPLE

PAIN	ANNOYANCE	EMBARRASSMENT	DIFFICULTY	TOTAL POINTS OUT OF 40
9	10	8	9	36

DEFINITION

Purple Nurple (*'pur-pel nur-pel*): The grabbing and twisting of a person's nipple in a forceful manner; also known as a Titty Twister.

TIPS FOR EXECUTION

☞ Grab the nipple with the thumb and forefinger rather than the entire hand as this will concentrate activity in the most sensitive area.

☞ Make sure to repeat the twisting motion several times in rapid succession to heighten discoloration; nothing is worse to the roguery connoisseur than a Lavender or a Magenta Nurple.

☞ In an era of heightened political correctness, consider asking the victim to sign a waiver; note that this should be done after the Purple Nurple, as the preemptive presentation of legal documentation may ruin the element of surprise necessary for success.

POSSIBLE COUNTERMEASURES

☞ If the perpetrator approaches from the front, place an elbow (on the side under assault) against the assailant's forearm and push forcibly outward. Note: this may cause pain to the victim as the Nurple is abruptly ended.

PURPLE NURPLE

☞ Again, for frontal attacks, grab the back of the assailant's head, typically with the weak side arm (i.e., the arm opposite the nipple under attack), pull it forward and render a Head Butt.

☞ For assaults from behind, see Atomic Wedgie countermeasures.

☞ For females or progressively minded males, a sturdy 1950's era brassiere will provide a foolproof defense; look in Grandma's closet for spares.

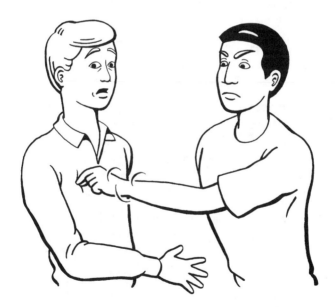

RAT TAIL

PAIN	ANNOYANCE	EMBARRASSMENT	DIFFICULTY	TOTAL POINTS OUT OF 40
10	9	9	7	35

DEFINITION

Rat Tail (*rat tAl*): Snapping the end of a large towel in a whip-like motion to inflict a welt on the skin of a nearby victim.

TIPS FOR EXECUTION

☞ Choose a weapon wisely; generally speaking, the larger the towel, the better, as greater length extends the striking radius.

☞ Don't super-size it; enormous beach towels may yield a roll so long as to become cumbersome and unwieldy (The Willard Effect).

☞ If time permits, prepare the weapon according to generally accepted best practices: 1) lay the towel flat on the ground. 2) fold one corner inward and across until it touches the opposite side. 3) roll inward from the new diagonal fold that has been created in step 2. The result should be a tight roll with a pointed end.

☞ For maximum pain, dip the tip in a swimming pool or other nearby water source; many experts believe that this will hold the tip in place and prevent unraveling.

☞ Aim for the victim's butt or leg using a quick snap of the wrist. Avoid the head and private parts to reduce risk of litigation.

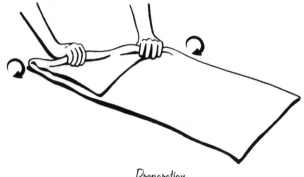

Preparation

Preparation (Optional)

RAT TAIL

POSSIBLE COUNTERMEASURES

☞ Be especially wary around swimming pools, locker rooms, and showers; any water source with towels nearby represents a serious Rat Tail hazard.

☞ If you are pursued in the open, running can be a good defense—unless you are wearing flip-flops.

☞ If on the run, avoid corners where one can get penned in and rat-tailed mercilessly.

☞ Although counter-intuitive, the best defensive maneuver when under attack is to move inward toward the assailant. Within one foot of the perpetrator lies the "eye" of the Rat Tail's "hurricane"—too close for a successful whip to be unleashed.

☞ Some highly trained defenders have been known to use their own towels to trap the perpetrator's extended Rat Tail, twisting it into a towel-lock and rendering the weapon useless. Successfully executed, this is way-cool, as it thoroughly embarrasses the assailant.

RAT TAIL

Execution

REVOLVING DOOR HOLD

PAIN	ANNOYANCE	EMBARRASSMENT	DIFFICULTY	TOTAL POINTS OUT OF 40
5	9	9	5	28

DEFINITION

Revolving Door Hold (*ri-'välv-ing dur hOld*): Entering a revolving door in the slot following someone else, then yanking the handle so as to stop the door's revolution; as a consequence of the revolving door hold, the person in the preceding slot will be carried by momentum into the door, often hitting it face first.

TIPS FOR EXECUTION

☞ Best execution occurs when the victim is in a hurry, thus speeding momentum.

☞ Ensure that no one else is in the revolving door at the time of execution, so as to minimize collateral damage.

POSSIBLE COUNTERMEASURES

☞ If suspicious of possible Revolving Door Hold, enter the apparatus after suspected assailant; only a Master Door Holder—or a very foolish one—will attempt to execute the act on a rear victim.

☞ Walk slowly through all revolving doors, with one or two hands on the door handle, to brace against sudden stoppage.

REVOLVING DOOR HOLD

☞ Many establishments with revolving doors also provide non-revolving alternatives; use these. Be aware, however, of the Door Jam.

SCOOP-A-LOOP

PAIN	ANNOYANCE	EMBARRASSMENT	DIFFICULTY	TOTAL POINTS OUT OF 40
2	6	6	7	21

DEFINITION

Scoop-a-Loop (*sküp A lüp*): Preventing the forward movement of another person by threading a forefinger through the victim's belt loop.

TIPS FOR EXECUTION

☞ Avoid attacks on running individuals for two reasons:
1) their speed makes it difficult to scoop the loop.
2) their momentum puts added stress on the index finger.

☞ Simple physics is the Scoop-a-Looper's best friend, so be sure to distribute stopping power evenly across the victim's waist. For single-finger Scoop-a-Loops, choose the middle back belt loop of the victim. Double Scoops involve both index fingers and should target the back belt loops to the immediate right and left of the middle back loop.

☞ For a hall of fame act of roguery, try the Scoop-a-Loop/Pants Yank combo.

POSSIBLE COUNTERMEASURES

☞ Always wear belts with pants that include loops.

☞ Test the clearance between belt and loops regularly; if the opening is too large, upgrade to a thicker belt.

☞ If scooped while walking, try to maintain some forward momentum, then twist and sprint at a 90-degree angle to the left. This unexpected move will trap a right-handed assailant's finger in the loop and hyper-extend the wrist and forearm (it goes without saying that, should the perpetrator be a known lefty, the twist and sprint should be flipped in the opposite direction).

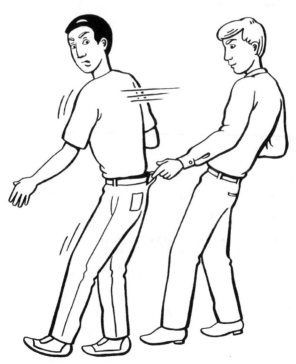

SHOE TIE

PAIN	ANNOYANCE	EMBARRASSMENT	DIFFICULTY	TOTAL POINTS OUT OF 40
3	7	9	6	25

DEFINITION

Shoe Tie (*'shü tl*): The tying of a person's shoes worn on both feet into a single knot, so as to immobilize the victim.

TIPS FOR EXECUTION

☞ Brute force is typically required, as the element of surprise is lessened by two factors: 1) the time required to execute the shoe tie. 2) the likelihood that the victim's feet are most often within the victim's visual range.

☞ Stage a diversion that will keep the victim's attention focused upward, such as a sky writer or Blue Angels fly-over.

☞ If the victim looks down in mid-execution, consider converting the act of roguery into a modified Nose Tweak or Ottoman.

POSSIBLE COUNTERMEASURES

☞ Kick the feet out in a bicycle motion.

☞ A kneeling perpetrator is a wonderful target for the Pants Yank or Atomic Wedgie.

☞ For complete protection against the Shoe Tie, wear loafers, sandals, or sneakers employing Velcro.

SHORT SHEET

PAIN	ANNOYANCE	EMBARRASSMENT	DIFFICULTY	TOTAL POINTS OUT OF 40
2	8	7	2	19

DEFINITION

Short Sheet (*short shEt*): Making a person's bed so that the top sheet is folded in half and tucked into the bed halfway to the foot of the mattress, so that the victim is unable to extend legs beyond the midpoint of the bed.

TIPS FOR EXECUTION

☞ Pay special attention to the quality of the made bed before remaking with a Short Sheet; a messy victim, for example, will immediately be suspicious of hospital corners.

☞ Make sure the top sheet is tucked in tightly; a loose fit will allow the victim to simply kick free of the Short Sheet.

☞ Pick targets carefully; short victims may not even realize they have been Short Sheeted.

☞ If in a camp or dorm setting, employ infrared goggles (if practical) to observe the victim's facial expressions.

POSSIBLE COUNTERMEASURES

☞ Pull the legs into a tuck position and kick up and out at a 45 degree angle to loosen the sheet.

☞ Many people actually prefer to sleep in the ball position; the Short Sheet may be the perfect excuse to try it.

SHORT SHEET

☞ Unless one person has saved another's life or has loaned him a large sum of money, it is unusual for someone to offer to make another person's bed; treat any such offers suspiciously.

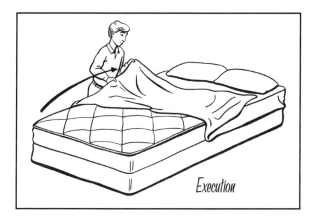

Execution

Result

SHOULDER TAP

PAIN	ANNOYANCE	EMBARRASSMENT	DIFFICULTY	TOTAL POINTS OUT OF 40
1	9	3	4	17

DEFINITION

Shoulder Tap (*shOl-der tap*): From a position next to a person, reaching behind and around to touch the opposite shoulder so as to dupe the victim into turning in the direction of the tap, where either no one or an unsuspecting third party awaits; the shoulder tap is similar in execution and annoyance to the Mosquito Flick.

TIPS FOR EXECUTION

☞ The Shoulder Tap is best carried out by long-armed people who are better able to reach across the length of the victim's back.

☞ Alternatively, short-armed people intent on executing the Shoulder Tap should seek out narrow-backed victims.

POSSIBLE COUNTERMEASURES

☞ The Shoulder Tap is difficult to avoid, as a person's natural inclination is to turn when summoned (see: FISP); the best defense, when tapped, is to simply respond verbally—with no movement—with a "Yes?" or a "What?"

SHOULDER TAP

☞ A Bowflex or other weight-training apparatus can help build deltoid muscle mass, thus increasing the surface area a Shoulder Tapper must cover to execute this act successfully.

☞ Women can both make a fashion statement and protect against the Shoulder Tap by sewing in shoulder pads specially designed to dampen any tapping activity.

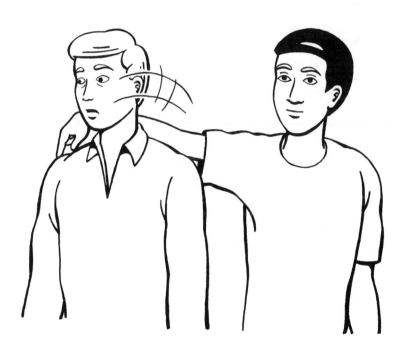

SODA EXPLODA

PAIN	ANNOYANCE	EMBARRASSMENT	DIFFICULTY	TOTAL POINTS OUT OF 40
2	7	8	1	18

DEFINITION

Soda Exploda (*sO-da ik-'splOda*): Shaking a carbonated beverage can to the point that it explodes when opened by an unsuspecting party; note that certain regions (chiefly Pittsburgh, Milwaukee, and the greater Willamette Valley) refer to this as the Pop Top.

TIPS FOR EXECUTION

☞ It is imperative to shake the can away from the victim's field of view; nothing is more embarrassing than a self-inflicted Soda Exploda (a.k.a. Fresca's Revenge).

☞ For optimal results, can should be between 55 and 62 degrees, and the number of shakes should be over 19.

☞ Use fresh cans to ensure proper carbonation. As a tip, most beverages now sport a "born on" date.

☞ Ideal victims include the fancily dressed (wedding party guests), the particularly parched (triathletes), and authority figures (school principals or office supervisors).

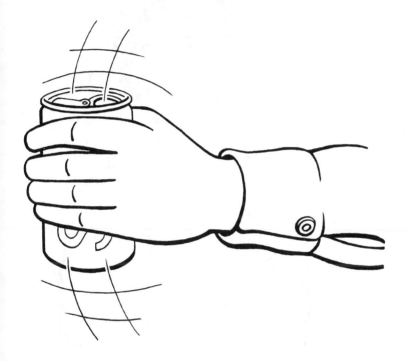

Execution

Result

SODA EXPLODA

POSSIBLE COUNTERMEASURES

☞ If offered a soda, be appreciative but wary; open the can at such an angle that the top faces the giver or a neutral territory.

☞ Junk science and pop culture have suggested that tapping the top of the can before opening will diffuse possible Sodas Explodas; laboratory research remains inconclusive at the time of printing.

☞ Beg off opening the can due to short finger nails or arthritis; if the giver refuses to open the can, assume the Soda Exploda is in play.

☞ Carbonated beverages can raise sodium levels and blood pressure; drink green tea or water as an alternative.

SPITBALL

PAIN	ANNOYANCE	EMBARRASSMENT	DIFFICULTY	TOTAL POINTS OUT OF 40
2	8	8	5	23

DEFINITION

Spitball (*spit bal*): Salivating on a small, wadded piece of paper, then using a straw or other projectile instrument to blow the ball at a person.

TIPS FOR EXECUTION

☞ Common reasons for CSBM (Catastrophic Spitball Malfunction) include over-saturating the ball, using an oversized piece of paper to form the wad, and miscalculating the firing range of the straw.

☞ Much as the inkwell of a disposable ball-point pen can serve as a breathing tube in an emergency tracheotomy, it may also be used in place of the Spitball straw if absolutely necessary.

☞ Despite the obvious temptation, do not inhale deeply immediately prior to firing. While doing so may provide extra force on the exhale, the risk of accidentally swallowing the ammunition will increase dramatically.

POSSIBLE COUNTERMEASURES

☞ When at all possible, sit or stand against a wall; only the most brazen Spitballer will launch a frontal assault.

SPITBALL

☞ Long sleeves and turtlenecks will cover many vulnerable target areas.

☞ A football helmet or catcher's mask is virtually impenetrable as head defense; however, in some situations this bulky headgear may prove awkward (such as the library, company board meetings, or Red Lobster restaurants).

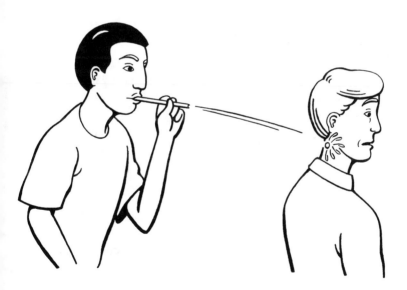

STRENGTH TEST

PAIN	ANNOYANCE	EMBARRASSMENT	DIFFICULTY	TOTAL POINTS OUT OF 40
5	7	7	6	25

DEFINITION

Strength Test (*strengkth test*): Clenching a person's hand and asking him or her to bend the arm at the elbow and resist as hard as possible while that hand is clenched and pulled in the opposite direction, so as to prove who is stronger; during the pulling and resistance, letting go suddenly so that the victim ends up striking his or her own face with the clenched fist.

TIPS FOR EXECUTION

☞ The harder the perpetrator pulls, the harder the victim will resist, and the greater the force of the retracting blow; use both hands to pull very hard downward on the victim's hand.

☞ During the exercise, be sure to egg on victims by telling them they are not doing well in the Strength Test; tell them octogenarian grandmothers can pull harder than they can.

☞ It is critical to pull for between seven and 12 seconds only. With less time, the victim has not built up full resistance pressure. With more time, the victim will be too fatigued to provide a powerful self-inflicted blow.

Execution

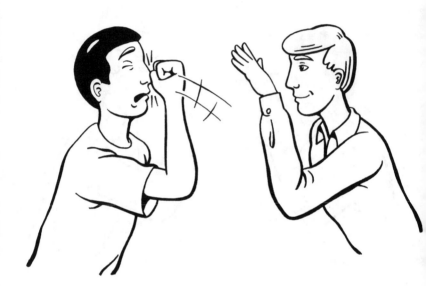

Result

STRENGTH TEST

POSSIBLE COUNTERMEASURES

☞ Play along with minimal pulling, but shake the affected arm as if exerting massive force; when the perpetrator releases the grip, use the affected arm or the other arm to deliver a slap to the face (a Backfire).

☞ Turn the tables by asking the prospective assailant to take the test first; in general, be suspicious of anyone who refuses to take a test that he is advocating for other people.

☞ Offer to partake in alternative, less-dangerous displays of arm strength like thumb wrestling, distance Frisbee throwing, or ripping small phone books in half.

URINAL GREETING

PAIN	ANNOYANCE	EMBARRASSMENT	DIFFICULTY	TOTAL POINTS OUT OF 40
1	10	10	3	24

DEFINITION

Urinal Greeting (*yur-en-nal grEting*): Greeting a fellow restroom patron with a slap on the back while he is urinating, so as to cause spray in unintended directions.

TIPS FOR EXECUTION

☞ Wait until the sound of urination is heard before commencing the greeting; once the victim starts peeing, it will be difficult for him to stop midstream.

☞ Sway the victim enough to the point where he feels he is losing control, but not so hard as to make a huge mess in the lavatory.

☞ Mix it up with a Knee Bend, or an Atomic Wedgie if you are feeling especially frisky.

☞ Shout "How the heck are ya, buddy?" the entire time, while keeping sure to remain outside the "lateral spray zone."

☞ Crowded restrooms (e.g., stadiums, airports, business conventions) can heighten the embarrassment factor.

POSSIBLE COUNTERMEASURES

☞ Stalls add privacy and allow one to lock out any potential intruders.

URINAL GREETING

☞ Keep one hand free during urination; this practice provides both a guard against would-be attackers and has the fringe benefit of cutting hand-washing time.

☞ A sharp turn toward the assailant during the Urinal Greeting (The Golden Shoe Shine) will provide a moist reminder that some acts of roguery carry a bad risk-to-reward ratio.

WARM WATER MANICURE

PAIN	ANNOYANCE	EMBARRASSMENT	DIFFICULTY	TOTAL POINTS OUT OF 40
1	9	10	5	25

DEFINITION

Warm Water Manicure (*worm wä-ter man-i-kyur*):
Placing a sleeping person's hand in a bowl of warm water in order to cause urination.

TIPS FOR EXECUTION

☞ It must be said that the Warm Water Manicure's effectiveness is rooted less in science than in summer camp folk legend.

☞ Patience is the manicurist's friend; it may take several hours of hand-soaking to lead to pants-soaking.

☞ In order to verify the Warm Water Manicure's success, someone must actually check for crotch dampness; as such, it is best to have an "associate" (e.g., a little brother or intern) available for such an inspection.

POSSIBLE COUNTERMEASURES

☞ Relieving oneself immediately prior to bedtime is a good prevention technique against both the Warm Water Manicure and the occasional nighttime accident.

☞ Rubber or latex gloves such as those used during dishwashing chores, though awkward to sleep with, should keep out water and prevent successful execution.

WARM WATER MANICURE

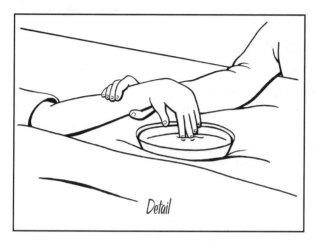

Detail

Overview

WET WILLIE

PAIN	ANNOYANCE	EMBARRASSMENT	DIFFICULTY	TOTAL POINTS OUT OF 40
3	10	9	8	30

DEFINITION

Wet Willie (*wet wi-lE*): The sequential actions of licking one's finger, sticking it in a victim's ear, and wiggling it as much as possible inside the ear canal; Double Wet Willies involve a simultaneous strike in both ears.

TIPS FOR EXECUTION

☞ As the goal is to get as much moisture into the ear as possible, saturate the strike finger with saliva.

☞ Minimize the amount of airtime and the exposure to non-target surfaces to avoid drying out finger; the entire cycle from finger extraction to successful placement should take no longer than 6 seconds (more time may be permissible in tropical or humid climates).

☞ For smaller victims or those with smaller ear openings, use the pinky as the strike finger; otherwise, the index finger is best due to its strength and dexterity.

☞ Never use the thumb or ring fingers, as they are too fat and too uncoordinated, respectively.

☞ Finger should aim for the center of the orifice and enter quickly and decisively; the element of surprise may be a useful component for execution.

WET WILLIE

☞ For maximum effect, cradle opposite side of victim's head with the non-striking hand or arm during the attack; propping up the head in this manner will cut down on victim's wiggle room, and should allow for deeper penetration as a result.

Step 1

⟹

WET WILLIE

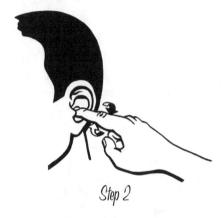

Step 2

POSSIBLE COUNTERMEASURES

☞ Earmuffs or hunters caps with flaps deployed will eliminate access to the targets.

☞ If an attack is imminent, stalling for time by running away or struggling may cause the finger to dry; alternatively, try blowing on the strike finger.

☞ If the perpetrator comes into contact, immediately shrug shoulder and tilt head into the attack side to pin perpetrator's hand/finger between the cheek and shoulder; alternatively, pivot entire body away from perpetrator and run away (preferably toward a Kleenex box).

☞ In case of Double Willie, same countermeasures apply, but pick a side to defend first.